9/20/68

Bev —

Happy, happy birth-
day! May your
20th year be filled
with much PEACE,
LOVE, Joy, & HAPPINESS!

Shalom —
Cathy.

D1112477

LOVE IS A POEM

WITH DECORATIONS BY
RUTH McCREA

· · ·

THE PETER PAUPER PRESS
Mount Vernon, New York

Love is a Poem

A GATHERING FROM THE POETS
WITH EXTRACTS FROM
SHAKESPEARE

LOVE IS A POEM

ARISE, MY LOVE

THE voice of my belovèd! behold, he cometh,
Leaping upon the mountains, skipping upon the hills.
My belovèd is like a roe or a young hart:
Behold, he standeth behind our wall,
He looketh in at the windows,
He showeth himself through the lattice.
My belovèd spoke, and said unto me,
"Rise up, my love, my fair one, and come away.
For, lo, the winter is past,
The rain is over and gone:
The flowers appear on the earth;
The time of the singing of birds is come,
And the voice of the turtle is heard in our land;
The fig tree ripeneth her green figs,
And the vines are in blossom,
They give forth their fragrance.

5

Arise, my love, my fair one, and come away.
O my dove, that art in the clefts of the rock,
    in the covert of the steep place,
Let me see thy countenance, let me hear
    thy voice;
For sweet is thy voice, and thy countenance
    is comely."

King Solomon

SET ME AS A SEAL

SET me as a seal upon thine heart;
As a seal upon thine arm:
For love is strong as death;
Jealousy is cruel as the grave,
The flashes thereof are flashes of fire,
A very flame of the Lord.
Many waters cannot quench love,
Neither can the floods drown it. . . .

King Solomon

A BOOK OF VERSES
UNDERNEATH THE BOUGH

A BOOK of Verses underneath the Bough,
A Jug of Wine, a Loaf of Bread — and Thou
Beside me singing in the Wilderness —
Oh, Wilderness were Paradise enow!

Some for the Glories of this World; and some
Sigh for the Prophet's Paradise to come;
Ah, take the Cash, and let the Credit go,
Nor heed the rumble of a distant Drum!

Would but some wingèd Angel ere too late
Arrest the yet unfolded Roll of Fate
And make the stern Recorder otherwise
Enregister, or quite obliterate!

Ah Love, could you and I with Him conspire
To grasp this sorry Scheme of Things entire,
Would not we shatter it to bits — and then
Remould it nearer to the Heart's desire!

Omar Khayyam

SHALL I COMPARE THEE

SHALL I compare thee to a summer's day?
Thou art more lovely and more temperate:
Rough winds do shake the darling buds of May,
And summer's lease hath all too short a date:
Sometimes too hot the eye of heaven shines,
And often is his gold complexion dimmed:
And every fair from fair sometime declines,
By chance, or nature's changing course, untrimmed.
But thy eternal summer shall not fade,
Nor lose possession of that fair thou ow'st,
Nor shall death brag thou wander'st in his shade,
When in eternal lines to time thou grow'st;
So long as men can breathe, or eyes can see,
So long lives this, and this gives life to thee.

William Shakespeare

Love like a shadow flies when substance love pursues;
Pursuing that that flies, and flying what pursues.

The Merry Wives of Windsor

'TIS EASY TO BE TRUE

NOT Celia, that I juster am,
Or better, than the rest;
For I would change each hour like them,
Were not my heart at rest.

But I am tied to very thee
By every thought I have:
Thy face I only care to see,
Thy heart I only crave.

All that in woman is adored
In thy dear self I find;
For the whole sex can but afford
The handsome and the kind.

Why then should I seek further store,
And still make love anew?
When change itself can give no more,
'Tis easy to be true!

Charles Sedley

TO ALTHEA
FROM PRISON

WHEN love with unconfinèd wings
Hovers within my gates,
And my divine Althea brings
To whisper at the grates;
When I lie tangled in her hair
And fettered to her eye,
The gods that wanton in the air
Know no such liberty.

When flowing cups run swiftly round,
With no allaying Thames,
Our careless heads with roses bound,
Our hearts with loyal flames;
When thirsty grief in wine we steep,
When healths and draughts go free,
Fishes that tipple in the deep
Know no such liberty.

When, like committed linnets, I
With shriller throat shall sing
The sweetness, mercy, majesty,
And glories of my king;
When I shall voice aloud, how good
He is, how great should be,
Enlargèd winds that curl the flood
Know no such liberty.

Stone walls do not a prison make,
Nor iron bars a cage;
Minds innocent and quiet take
That for an hermitage.
If I have freedom in my love,
And in my soul am free,
Angels alone that soar above
Enjoy such liberty.

Richard Lovelace

O MISTRESS MINE

O MISTRESS mine, where are you roaming?
O, stay and hear! your true love's coming,
That can sing both high and low:
Trip no further, pretty sweeting;
Journeys end in lovers meeting;
Every wise man's son doth know.

What is love? 'Tis not hereafter;
Present mirth hath present laughter;
What's to come is still unsure:
In delay there lies no plenty;
Then come kiss me, sweet and twenty,
Youth's a stuff will not endure.

William Shakespeare

If thou remember'st not the slightest folly
That ever love did make thee run into,
Thou hast not loved.

As You Like It

TAKE, O TAKE, THOSE LIPS AWAY

TAKE, O take, those lips away,
That so sweetly were forsworn!
And those eyes, the break of day,
Lights that do mislead the morn!
But my kisses bring again —
Seals of love, but sealed in vain.

Hide, O hide, those hills of snow,
Which thy frozen bosom bears,
On whose tops the pinks that grow
Are of those that April wears!
But first set my poor heart free,
Bound in those icy chains by thee.

Shakespeare and Fletcher

Love is a spirit all compact of fire,
Not gross to sink, but light, and will aspire.

Venus and Adonis

GATHER YE ROSEBUDS

GATHER ye rosebuds while ye may,
Old Time is still a-flying:
And this same flower that smiles today
Tomorrow will be dying.

The glorious lamp of heaven, the sun,
The higher he's a-getting,
The sooner will his race be run,
And nearer he's to setting.

That age is best which is the first,
When youth and blood are warmer;
But being spent, the worse, and worst
Times still succeed the former.

Then be not coy, but use your time,
And while ye may, go marry:
For having lost but once your prime,
You may for ever tarry.

Robert Herrick

THE PASSIONATE SHEPHERD TO HIS LOVE

COME live with me and be my Love,
And we will all the pleasures prove
That hills and valleys, dales and fields,
Or woods or steepy mountain yields.

And we will sit upon the rocks,
And see the shepherds feed their flocks
By shallow rivers, to whose falls
Melodious birds sing madrigals.

And I will make thee beds of roses
And a thousand fragrant posies;
A cap of flowers, and a kirtle
Embroidered all with leaves of myrtle.

A gown made of the finest wool
Which from our pretty lambs we pull;
Fair-lined slippers for the cold,
With buckles of the purest gold.

A belt of straw and ivy-buds
With coral clasps and amber studs;
And if these pleasures may thee move,
Come live with me and be my Love.

The shepherd swains shall dance and sing
For thy delight each May morning;
If these delights thy mind may move,
Come live with me and be my Love.

Christopher Marlowe

This is the very ecstasy of love,
Whose violent property fordoes itself
And leads the will to desperate undertakings
As oft as any passion under heaven
That does afflict our natures.

Hamlet

SONG – TO CELIA

DRINK to me only with thine eyes
And I will pledge with mine
Or leave a kiss but in the cup
And I'll not look for wine.
The thirst that from the soul doth rise
Doth ask a drink divine
But might I of Jove's nectar sup
I would not change for thine.

I sent thee late a rosy wreath,
Not so much honoring thee
As giving it a hope that there
It could not withered be.
But thou thereon didst only breathe
And send'st it back to me:
Since when it grows, and smells, I swear,
Not of itself but thee.

Ben Jonson

CUPID AND CAMPASPE

CUPID and my Campaspe played
At cards for kisses. Cupid paid;
He stakes his quiver, bow, and arrows,
His mother's doves, and team of sparrows;
Loses them too; then, down he throws
The coral of his lip, the rose
Growing on's cheek (but none knows how)
With these, the crystal of his brow,
And then the dimple of his chin;
All these did my Campaspe win.
At last he set her both his eyes;
She won, and Cupid blind did rise.
O Love! has she done this to thee?
What shall (alas!) become of me?

John Lyly

They say, base men being in love have then
a nobility in their natures more than is native
to them.

Othello

SEND BACK MY HEART

I PRYTHEE send me back my heart,
Since I can not have thine:
For if from yours you will not part,
Why then should'st thou have mine?

Yet now I think on't, let it lie;
To find it were in vain,
For thou'st a thief in either eye
Would steal it back again.

Why should two hearts in one breast lie,
And yet not lodge together?
Oh Love! where is thy sympathy,
If thus our breasts thou sever?

But love is such a mystery,
I cannot find it out:
For when I think I'm best resolved,
I then am in most doubt.

Then farewell care, and farewell woe,
I will no longer pine;
For I'll believe I have her heart
As much as she has mine.

John Suckling

LOVE, BUT KNOW NOT WHY

LOVE not me for comely grace,
For my pleasing eye or face,
Nor for any outward part;
No, nor for my constant heart:
For those may fail or turn to ill, —
So thou and I shall sever.

Keep therefore a true woman's eye,
And love me still, but know not why:
So hast thou the same reason still
To doat upon me ever.

Anonymous

TO LUCASTA

TELL me not, Sweet, I am unkind
That from the nunnery
Of thy chaste breast, and quiet mind,
To war and arms I fly.

True, a new mistress now I chase,
The first foe in the field;
And with a stronger faith embrace
A sword, a horse, a shield.

Yet this inconstancy is such
As you too shall adore;
I could not love thee, Dear, so much,
Loved I not honor more.

Richard Lovelace

Love is too young to know what conscience is;
Yet who knows not conscience is born of love?

Shakespeare's Sonnets

23

O MY LUVE IS LIKE
A RED, RED ROSE

O MY Luve is like a red, red rose
That's newly sprung in June:
O my Luve is like the melodie
That's sweetly play'd in tune.

As fair art thou, my bonnie lass,
So deep in luve am I:
And I will luve thee still, my dear,
Till a' the seas gang dry.

Till a' the seas gang dry, my dear,
And the rocks melt wi' the sun:
And I will luve thee still, my dear,
While the sands o' life shall run.

And fare thee weel, my only Luve,
And fare thee weel a while!
And I will come again, my Luve,
Tho' it were ten thousand mile.

Robert Burns

BELIEVE ME, IF ALL THOSE
ENDEARING YOUNG CHARMS

BELIEVE me, if all those endearing young charms
Which I gaze on so fondly today
Were to fade by tomorrow and fleet in my arms
Like fairy gifts fading away,
Thou wouldst still be adored as this moment thou art,
Let thy loveliness fade as it will,
And around the dear ruin each wish of my heart
Would entwine itself verdantly still.

It is not while beauty and youth are thine own
And thy cheeks unprofaned by a tear
That the fervor and faith of a soul can be known
To which time will but make thee more dear.
No, the heart that has truly loved never forgets
But as truly loves on to the close —
As the sunflower turns on her god when he sets
The same look which she turned when he rose.

Thomas Moore

NEVER SEEK TO TELL

NEVER seek to tell thy love,
Love that never told can be;
For the gentle wind does move
Silently, invisibly.

I told my love, I told my love,
I told her all my heart,
Trembling, cold, in ghastly fears.
Ah, she did depart!

Soon as she was gone from me
A traveler came by
Silently, invisibly.
— He took her with a sigh.

William Blake

Doubt that the stars are fire;
Doubt that the sun doth move;
Doubt truth to be a liar;
But never doubt I love.

Hamlet

LUCY

SHE dwelt among the untrodden ways
Beside the springs of Dove,
A maid whom there were none to praise,
And very few to love.

A violet by a mossy stone
Half-hidden from the eye!
— Fair as a star, when only one
Is shining in the sky.

She lived unknown, and few could know
When Lucy ceased to be;
But she is in her grave, and, oh,
The difference to me!

. . .

I travel'd among unknown men,
In lands beyond the sea;
Nor, England, did I know till then
What love I bore to thee.

'Tis past, that melancholy dream!
Nor will I quit thy shore
A second time; for still I seem
To love thee more and more.

Among thy mountains did I feel
The joy of my desire;
And she I cherished turned her wheel
Beside an English fire.

Thy morning show'd, thy nights conceal'd
The bowers where Lucy play'd;
And thine too is the last green field
That Lucy's eyes survey'd.

William Wordsworth

SHE WAS A PHANTOM
OF DELIGHT

SHE was a phantom of delight
When first she gleam'd upon my sight;
A lovely Apparition, sent

To be a moment's ornament;
Her eyes as stars of twilight fair;
Like Twilight's, too, her dusky hair;
But all things else about her drawn
From May-time and the cheerful dawn;
A dancing shape, an image gay,
To haunt, to startle, and waylay.

I saw her upon nearer view,
A Spirit, yet a Woman too!
Her household motions light and free,
And steps of virgin-liberty;
A countenance in which did meet
Sweet records, promises as sweet;
A creature not too bright or good
For human nature's daily food,
For transient sorrows, simple wiles,
Praise, blame, love, kisses, tears, and smiles.

And now I see with eye serene
The very pulse of the machine;

TO ——

ONE word is too often profaned
For me to profane it,
One feeling too falsely disdained
For thee to disdain it;
One hope is too like despair
For prudence to smother,
And pity from thee more dear
Than that from another.

I can give not what men call love,
But wilt thou accept not
The worship the heart lifts above
And the Heavens reject not, —
The desire of the moth for the star,
Of the night for the morrow,
The devotion to something afar
From the sphere of our sorrow?

Percy Bysshe Shelley

A being breathing thoughtful breath,
A traveler between life and death:
The reason firm, the temperate will,
Endurance, foresight, strength, and skill;
A perfect Woman, nobly plann'd,
To warn, to comfort, and command;
And yet a Spirit still, and bright
With something of an angel-light.

William Wordsworth

LOVE'S BLINDNESS

I HAVE heard of reasons manifold
Why love must needs be blind,
But this the best of all I hold, —
His eyes are in his mind.
What outward form and feature are
He guesseth but in part;
But what within is good and fair
He seeth with the heart.

Samuel Taylor Coleridge

LOVE'S PHILOSOPHY

THE fountains mingle with the river,
And the rivers with the Ocean,
The winds of Heaven mix for ever
With a sweet emotion;
Nothing in the world is single;
All things by a law divine
In one spirit meet and mingle.
Why not I with thine?

See the mountains kiss high Heaven
And the waves clasp one another;
No sister flower would be forgiven
If it disdained its brother;
And the sunlight clasps the earth
And the moonbeams kiss the sea;
What is all this sweet work worth
If thou kiss not me?

                                   Percy Bysshe Shelley

THE INDIAN SERENADE

I ARISE from dreams of thee
In the first sweet sleep of night,
When the winds are breathing low,
And the stars are shining bright:
I arise from dreams of thee,
And a spirit in my feet
Hath led me — who knows how?
To thy chamber window, Sweet!

The wandering airs they faint
On the dark, the silent stream —
And the Champak's odors fail
Like sweet thoughts in a dream;
The nightingale's complaint,
It dies upon her heart; —
As I must on thine,
O! belovèd as thou art!

O lift me from the grass!
I die! I faint! I fail!

35

Let thy love in kisses rain
On my lips and eyelids pale.
My cheek is cold and white, alas!
My heart beats loud and fast; —
Oh! press it close to thine again,
Where it will break at last.

Percy Bysshe Shelley

TO ——

I FEAR thy kisses, gentle maiden,
Thou needest not fear mine;
My spirit is too deeply laden
Ever to burthen thine.

I fear thy mien, thy tones, thy motion,
Thou needest not fear mine;
Innocent is the heart's devotion
With which I worship thine.

Percy Bysshe Shelley

NOT IN THE WINTER

IT WAS not in the winter
Our loving lot was cast;
It was the time of roses, —
We plucked them as we passed!

That churlish season never frowned
On early lovers yet;
O no! — the world was newly crowned
With flowers when first we met.

'Twas twilight, and I bade you go;
But still you held me fast.
It was the time of roses, —
We plucked them as we passed!

Thomas Hood

Love is begun by time . . .
Time qualifies the spark and fire of it;
There lives within the very flame of love
A kind of wick or snuff that will abate it.

Hamlet

ANNABEL LEE

IT WAS many and many a year ago,
In a kingdom by the sea
That a maiden there lived whom you may know
By the name of Annabel Lee; —
And this maiden she lived with no other thought
Than to love and be loved by me.

I was a child and she was a child,
In this kingdom by the sea,
But we loved with a love that was more than love —
I and Annabel Lee —
With a love that the wingèd seraphs of Heaven
Coveted her and me.

And this was the reason that, long ago,
In this kingdom by the sea,
A wind blew out of a cloud, by night,
Chilling my Annabel Lee;
So that her high-born kinsmen came

And bore her away from me,
To shut her up in a sepulcher
In this kingdom by the sea.

The angels, not half so happy in Heaven,
Went envying her and me: —
Yes! — that was the reason (as all men know,
In this kingdom by the sea)
That the wind came out of the cloud, chilling
And killing my Annabel Lee.

But our love it was stronger by far than the love
Of those who were older than we —
Of many far wiser than we —
And neither the angels in Heaven above,
Nor the demons down under the sea,
Can ever dissever my soul from the soul
Of the beautiful Annabel Lee: —

For the moon never beams without bringing
    me dreams

Of the beautiful Annabel Lee;
And the stars never rise but I feel the bright eyes
Of the beautiful Annabel Lee;
And so, all the night-tide, I lie down by the side
Of my darling, — my darling, — my life and my
    bride,
In the sepulcher there by the sea —
In her tomb by the sounding sea.

Edgar Allan Poe

JENNY KISSED ME

JENNY kissed me when we met,
Jumping from the chair she sat in;
Time, you thief, who love to get
Sweets into your list, put that in!
Say I'm weary, say I'm sad,
Say that health and wealth have missed me,
Say I'm growing old, but add,
Jenny kissed me.

Leigh Hunt

CUPID SWALLOWED

T' OTHER day, as I was twining
Roses, for a crown to dine in,
What, of all things, midst the heap,
Should I light on, fast asleep,
But the little desperate elf,
The tiny traitor, — Love himself!
By the wings I pinched him up
Like a bee, and in a cup
Of my wine I plunged and sank him;
And what d'ye think I did? — I drank him!
Faith, I thought him dead. Not he!
There he lives with tenfold glee;
And now this moment, with his wings
I feel him tickling my heart strings.

Leigh Hunt

Love is blind and lovers cannot see
The pretty follies that themselves commit.

Merchant of Venice

TO HELEN

HELEN, thy beauty is to me
Like those Nicaean barks of yore,
That gently, o'er a perfumed sea,
The weary, wayworn wanderer bore
To his own native shore.

On desperate seas long wont to roam,
Thy hyacinth hair, thy classic face,
Thy Naiad airs, have brought me home
To the glory that was Greece
And the grandeur that was Rome.

Lo! in yon brilliant window-niche
How statue-like I see thee stand,
The agate lamp within thy hand!
As, Psyche, from the regions which
Are Holy Land!

Edgar Allan Poe

HOW DO I LOVE THEE?

How DO I love thee? Let me count the ways.
I love thee to the depth and breadth and height
My soul can reach, when feeling out of sight
For the ends of Being an ideal Grace.
I love thee to the level of everyday's
Most quiet need, by sun and candle-light.
I love thee freely, as men strive for Right;
I love thee purely, as they turn from Praise.
I love thee with the passion put to use
In my old griefs, and with my childhood's faith.
I love thee with a love I seemed to lose
With my lost saints, — I love thee with the breath,
Smiles, tears, of all my life! — and, if God choose,
I shall but love thee better after death.

Elizabeth Barrett Browning

O, 'tis a curse in love, and still approved,
When women cannot love where they're beloved!

Two Gentlemen of Verona

CYNARA

Last night, ah, yesternight, betwixt her lips and mine
There fell thy shadow, Cynara! thy breath was shed
Upon my soul between the kisses and the wine;
And I was desolate and sick of an old passion,
Yea, I was desolate and bowed my head:
I have been faithful to thee, Cynara! in my fashion.

All night upon mine heart I felt her warm heart beat,
Night-long within mine arms in love and sleep she lay;
Surely the kisses of her bought red mouth were sweet;
But I was desolate and sick of an old passion,
When I awoke and found the dawn was gray:
I have been faithful to thee, Cynara! in my fashion.

I have forgot much, Cynara! gone with the wind,
Flung roses, roses riotously with the throng,
Dancing, to put thy pale, lost lilies out of mind;
But I was desolate and sick of an old passion,
Yea, all the time, because the dance was long:
I have been faithful to thee, Cynara! in my fashion.

I cried for madder music and for stronger wine,
But when the feast is finished and the lamps expire,
Then falls thy shadow, Cynara! the night is thine;
And I am desolate and sick of an old passion,
Yea, hungry for the lips of my desire:
I have been faithful to thee, Cynara! in my fashion.

Ernest Dowson

    Here I prophesy:
Sorrow on love hereafter shall attend:
It shall be waited on with jealousy,
Find sweet beginning, but unsavory end. . . .
It shall suspect where is no cause of fear;
It shall not fear where it should most mistrust;
It shall be merciful and too severe,
And most deceiving when it seems most just.

Venus and Adonis

PARTING

MY LIFE closed twice before its close;
It yet remains to see
If Immortality unveil
A third event to me

So huge, so hopeless to conceive
As these that twice befell.
Parting is all we know of heaven
And all we need of hell.

Emily Dickinson

SLY THOUGHTS

"I SAW him kiss your cheek!" — "'Tis true."
"O Modesty!" — "'Twas strictly kept:
He thought me asleep; at least, I knew
He thought I thought he thought I slept."

Coventry Patmore

THE MILLER'S DAUGHTER

IT IS the miller's daughter,
And she is grown so dear, so dear,
That I would be the jewel
That trembles in her ear:
For hid in ringlets day and night,
I'd touch her neck so warm and white.

And I would be the girdle
About her dainty dainty waist,
And her heart would beat against me,
In sorrow and in rest;
And I should know if it beat right,
I'd clasp it round so close and tight.

And I would be the necklace,
And all day long to fall and rise
Upon her balmy bosom,
With her laughter or her sighs,
And I would lie so light, so light,
I scarce should be unclasp'd at night.

Alfred, Lord Tennyson

BEDOUIN SONG

FROM the desert I come to thee
On a stallion shod with fire;
And the winds are left behind
In the speed of my desire.
Under thy window I stand
And the midnight hears my cry:
I love thee, I love but thee,
With a love that cannot die
Till the sun grows cold,
And the stars are old,
And the leaves of the Judgment Book unfold!

Look from thy window and see
My passion and my pain;
I lie on the sands below
And I faint in thy disdain.
Let the night-winds touch thy brow
With the heat of my burning sigh,
And melt thee to hear the vow
Of a love that shall not die

Till the sun grows cold
And the stars are old
And the leaves of the Judgment Book unfold!

My steps are nightly driven
By the fever in my breast
To hear from thy lattice breathed
The word that shall give me rest.
Open the door of thy heart
And open thy chamber door,
And my kisses shall teach thy lips
The love that shall fade no more
Till the sun grows cold
And the stars are old
And the leaves of the Judgment Book unfold!

Bayard Taylor

Young men's love then lies
Not truly in their hearts, but in their eyes.

Romeo and Juliet

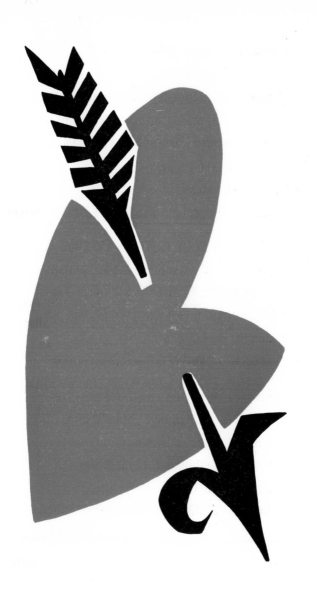

ECHO

COME to me in the silence of the night;
Come in the speaking silence of a dream;
Come with soft rounded cheeks and eyes as bright
As sunlight on a stream;
Come back in tears,
O memory, hope, love of finished years.

O dream how sweet, too sweet, too bitter-sweet,
Whose wakening should have been in Paradise,
Where souls brim-full of love abide and meet;
Where thirsty longing eyes
Watch the slow door
That opening, letting in, lets out no more.

Yet come to me in dreams, that I may live
My very life again though cold in death;
Come back to me in dreams, that I may give
Pulse for pulse, breath for breath:
Speak low, lean low,
As long ago my love, how long ago.

Christina Rossetti

YOU'LL LOVE ME YET!

YOU'LL love me yet! And I can tarry
Your love's protracted growing.
June reared that bunch of flowers you carry
From seeds of April's sowing.

I plant a heartful now; some seed
At least is sure to strike
And yield — what you'll not pluck indeed,
Not love, but, may be, like.

You'll look at least on love's remains,
A grave's one violet.
Your look? — that pays a thousand pains —
What's death! You'll love me yet!

Robert Browning

By heaven, I do love: and it hath taught me
to rhyme and to be melancholy.

Love's Labour's Lost

THE MOTH'S KISS FIRST

THE moth's kiss first!
Kiss me as if you made believe
You were not sure, this eve,
How my face, your flower, had pursed
Its petals up; so, here and there
You brush it, till I grow aware
Who wants me, and wide open burst.

The bee's kiss, now!
Kiss me as if you entered gay
My heart at some noonday, —
A bud that dares not disallow
The claim, so all is rendered up;
And passively its shattered cup
Over your head to sleep I bow.

Robert Browning

O, love's best habit is a soothing tongue.

The Passionate Pilgrim

IF THOU MUST LOVE ME

IF THOU must love me, let it be for nought
Except for love's sake only. Do not say
"I love her for her smile, . . . her look, . . . her way
Of speaking gently, . . . for a trick of thought
That falls in well with mine, and certes brought
A sense of pleasant ease on such a day" —
For these things in themselves, Belovèd, may
Be changed or change for thee, — and love so wrought
May be unwrought so. Neither love me for
Thine own dear pity's wiping my cheeks dry:
A creature might forget to weep, who bore
Thy comfort long, and lose thy love thereby.
But love me for love's sake, that evermore
Thou mays't love on through love's eternity.

Elizabeth Barrett Browning

She burn'd with love, as straw with fire flameth;
She burn'd out love, as soon as straw out-burneth.

The Passionate Pilgrim

ROSES

I HAVE placed a golden
Ring upon the hand
Of the blithest little
Lady in the land!

When the early roses
Scent the sunny air
She shall gather white ones
To tremble in her hair!

Hasten, happy roses!
Come to me by May!
In your folded petals
Lies my wedding-day.

Thomas Bailey Aldrich

Ah me! how sweet is love itself possess'd,
When but love's shadows are so rich in joy!

Romeo and Juliet

ALL THROUGH THE NIGHT

WHILE the Moon her watch is keeping,
All through the night —
While the weary world is sleeping,
All through the night —
O'er my bosom gently stealing,
Visions of delight revealing,
Breathes a pure and holy feeling,
All through the night.

Fondly then I dream of thee, Love —
All through the night:
Waking, still thy form I see, Love —
All through the night.
When this mortal coil is over,
Will thy gentle spirit hover
O'er the bed where sleeps thy lover —
All through the night?

Thomas Oliphant

AGRO-DOLCE

ONE kiss from all others prevents me,
And sets all my pulses astir,
And burns on my lips and torments me:
'Tis the kiss that I fain would give her.

One kiss for all others requites me,
Although it is never to be,
And sweetens my dreams and invites me:
'Tis the kiss that she dare not give me.

James Russell Lowell

I WAS A KING IN BABYLON

OR EVER the knightly years were gone
With the old world into the grave,
I was a King in Babylon
And you were a Christian slave.

I saw, I took, I cast you by;
I bent and broke your pride.
You loved me well — or I heard them lie —

56

But your longing was denied.
Surely I knew that by and by
You cursed your gods and died.

And a myriad suns have set and shone
Since those upon the grave
Decreed by the King of Babylon
To her that had been his slave.

The pride I trampled is now my scathe,
For it tramples me again.
The old resentment lasts like death
For you love, yet you refrain.
I break my heart on your hard unfaith
And I break my heart in vain.

Yet not for an hour do I wish undone
The deed beyond the grave
When I was a King in Babylon
And you were a virgin slave!

William Ernest Henley

WHEN I WAS
ONE-AND-TWENTY

WHEN I was one-and-twenty
I heard a wise man say,
"Give crowns and pounds and guineas
But not your heart away;
Give pearls away and rubies
But keep your fancy free."
But I was one-and-twenty,
No use to talk to me.

When I was one-and-twenty
I heard him say again,
"The heart out of the bosom
Was never given in vain;
'Tis paid with sighs a-plenty
And sold for endless rue."
And I am two-and-twenty,
And oh, 'tis true, 'tis true!

A. E. Housman

WHITE IN THE MOON

WHITE in the moon the long road lies,
The moon stands blank above;
White in the moon the long road lies
That leads me from my love.

Still hangs the hedge without a gust,
Still, still the shadows stay:
My feet upon the moonlit dust
Pursue the ceaseless way.

The world is round, so travelers tell,
And straight though reach the track,
Trudge on, trudge on, 'twill all be well,
The way will guide one back.

But ere the circle homeward hies
Far, far it must remove:
White in the moon the long road lies
That leads me from my love.

A. E. Housman